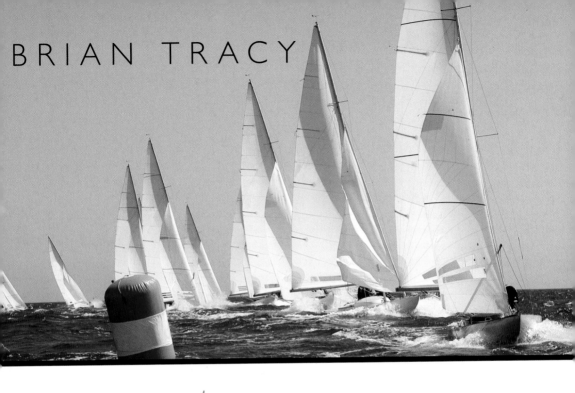

BRIAN TRACY

THE 7 SECRETS OF EXCEPTIONAL *Leadership*

Printed and bound in the United States of America

WOZ 10 9 8 7 6 5 4 3

TABLE OF CONTENTS

Introduction:

Your ability to take charge, to lead, to get the best out of yourself and others, is vital to your achieving your full potential in life.

The good news is that leaders are made, usually *self-made* through work on themselves, not born. Leadership is action, not position. It is defined by what you do, not by your title on your business card.

A leader is an executive. What is an executive? It is someone who executes, takes action, achieves goals and moves ahead. What this means is that you can be a leader without followers.

The definition of leadership is: "The ability to get results." When you think and act like a leader, you soon get the results that leaders get, and enjoy the results of leadership—respect, esteem, more opportunities, higher pay and a life of significance—making a real difference in your world. There is more good news. Leadership is not fixed. It is a set of learnable attitudes and skills. This means that you can *learn* any leadership skill you need to achieve any leadership goal that you can set for yourself.

How do top leaders think and act? In more than 3,300 studies of leaders over the centuries, "seven secrets of leadership" have been identified that you can learn and apply. But in reality, there are no real "secrets" of leadership. There are only timeless truths that have been discovered and rediscovered again and again over the centuries. Here they are:

Leaders Know Who They Are

Leaders have clarity. They know who they are and who they are not, and what they want and what they do not want.

Leaders know what they believe in, and what they do not believe in. They know what they stand for, and what they will not stand for.

Each leader is a distinct individual, distinct and different from all others. Leaders are not "like someone else," because each leader is in a category of one.

I believe in the adage: "Be yourself, everyone else is already taken." This is the attitude of the leader.

Inscribed over the temple of The Delphic Oracle, 2,500 years ago, were the words, "Man, Know Thyself."

Modern psychologists say the same thing. Leaders are superior individuals, self-actualizing people who are honest and objective with themselves. They know themselves and accept who they are, without apologies or defensiveness.

Leaders also have a clear idea of the people they would like to be in the *future*, their ideal image, toward which they continually strive in the process of self-improvement.

Because leaders have taken the time to look into themselves, to know themselves as they really are inside, leaders are not wishy-washy about what they like or dislike, want or do not want. They are clear and distinct.

Becoming an excellent leader, therefore, begins with you, with your developing complete clarity about yourself, and about what you think, feel and believe in.

The *Personality* of the *Leader*

Imagine that your personality is composed of a series of five concentric circles, like a dart board, starting with the bull's eye, the very heart and core of your personality. This axle around which your life turns, or central part of your character which determines the way you think and feel, is made up of your *values*—those virtues and aspects of life that are most important to you.

Leaders are clear about their values; non-leaders are unsure and vague. Leaders never compromise their core values. Followers modify or abandon their values whenever offered a reward or benefit of some kind.

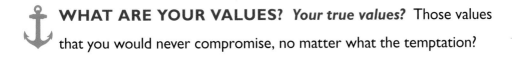

WHAT ARE YOUR VALUES? *Your true values?* Those values that you would never compromise, no matter what the temptation?

Your true values are only revealed under pressure, when you are forced to choose between one value or another. Your true values are only revealed in your actions, when there is a possibility of loss, especially financial loss, or of embarrassment, or experiencing the disapproval of one or more people. This is when you reveal your true values.

Do you believe in the values of honesty, love, family, freedom, courage and responsibility? If you do, you will always practice these values, no matter what happens around you.

What Do You *Believe?*

The second circle or layer of your personality is composed of your *beliefs*. What do you believe about yourself, about other people, about your potential, and about society?

Your beliefs grow out of your values, especially your beliefs about yourself. They determine your worldview—positive or negative.

Denis Waitley wrote,

"If you believe you can, you probably can. If you believe you won't, you most assuredly won't. Belief is the ignition switch that gets you off the launching pad."

Your positive, empowering beliefs about yourself, others and life are what make you a leader.

Your negative, self-limiting beliefs about yourself, or others, are what hold you back. What are they?

Expect the *Best*

The third circle of your personality is composed of your expectations. Your values and beliefs determine your expectations about your personal potential, the people around you, and the situation you are currently facing.

Leaders have clear, solid values that they live by every day. They have positive uplifting beliefs about themselves and what is possible for them. As a result, they have positive expectations.

Leaders confidently expect to be successful. If they fail temporarily, they confidently expect to learn something valuable that will help them in the future.

A Positive *Attitude*

The fourth layer of personality, determined by your values, beliefs and expectations, is your attitude. Earl Nightingale called attitude "the most important word in the language."

Leaders have a positive mental attitude. They see opportunities where others see problems. They see stepping stones where others see stumbling blocks.

They approach situations, people and life with the confident expectation that they will be successful, and that their companies, their products and services will be successful as well.

Action is Everything

The fifth layer of success, the natural extension of your values, beliefs, expectations and attitudes, are your actions—what you do each day.

You can always tell what is going on inside of a person by looking at their actions; at what they do, not what they say.

Emerson wrote,
"What you are shouts at me so loudly that I cannot hear a word you are saying."
The person you are inside as a leader is almost immediately obvious to all the people around you. It is almost impossible to hide.

Evaluate YOURSELF

Here is an exercise for you.

Complete these sentences:

   1) My true values are…

      (What are your three to five most important values or concerns in life?);

   2) What I believe about life and people is…
      (Based on your values, what do you believe about your world?);

   3) Life is…
      (How would you describe life in general?);

   4) What is most important to me is…

      (What are your most important goals in life, right now?).

How would the people around you describe you to others, based on their experiences with you, and with what you say and do day-to-day?

Most of all, if you could wave a magic wand and become your ideal of the perfect person, what qualities would you have?

What would you do or say differently in your interactions with others if you were already an exceptional leader?

Most of all, what are you going to be or do differently from now on in your commitment to be an exceptional leader, based on what you have learned in this chapter?

"Values are critical guides for making decisions. When in doubt, they cut through the fog like a beacon in the night."

ROBERT TOWNSEND

Leaders
Know What They Want

Leaders have definite, distinct personalities. They have qualities of strength, character and assurance about them that cause people to look up to them and respect them.

In addition to personal clarity, knowing who they are, leaders are clear about their *goals*. They know what they want, and are determined to get it.

Goal-orientation is the "master skill of success." It is the most outwardly identifiable quality of a leader or top performer. Fortunately, the ability to set and achieve goals is a learnable skill.

Achieving *Clarity*

There are several key questions that you need to ask and answer for yourself. These questions help you develop greater clarity about what you really want to achieve.

What are your three most important goals in life, right now? When you write down your answer in 30 seconds or less, you get an immediate snapshot of what is most important to you at the moment.

1. _____

2. _____

3. _____

What goals would you set for yourself, what would you want to do with your life, if you had 20 million dollars in the bank, but you only had ten years left to live?

This is another way of asking what you would want to be, have and do with your life if you had no financial limitations, if you were completely free to choose your future. How would you answer this question?

1. _____

2. _____

3. _____

What **one great goal** would you set for yourself if you knew you could not fail? Imagine that you could wave a magic wand and achieve any one goal in life, large or small, short-term or long-term. What goal would that be?

_____

_____

_____

_____

Whatever your answer to this question, the very fact that you could think about it and write it down means that it is probably possible for you. The only question is,

"How badly do you want it?"

And perhaps the most important question of all:
*"What do you **really want** to do with your life?"*

You were put on this earth to do something wonderful with your life. What could it be?

_____

_____

_____

_____

Once you are clear about your personal goals, you then ask, *"What are my three most important **business** goals, right now?"* The primary responsibility of leaders is to set and achieve business goals. What are yours?

1. _____

2. _____

3. _____

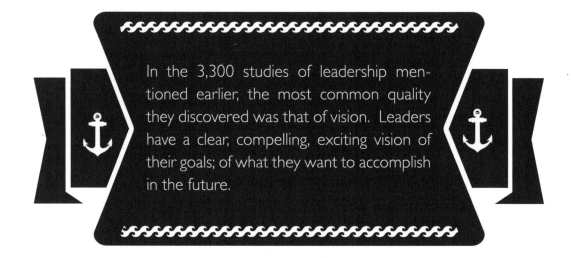

In the 3,300 studies of leadership mentioned earlier, the most common quality they discovered was that of vision. Leaders have a clear, compelling, exciting vision of their goals; of what they want to accomplish in the future.

Think About the *Future*

Leaders practice "future-orientation." They idealize and imagine they could create a perfect future for their company or department.

Leaders practice "back-from-the-future thinking." They project forward three to five years and imagine what their perfect business situation or career would look like, if they had no limitations.

They then look back from the vantage point of the future, in their mind, to their situation today and ask, "What would have to happen for me to start moving from where I am today to create my ideal future vision of tomorrow?"

If your future was perfect as a leader, if your company, department or area of responsibility was the best in the business, how would it be different from today? The greater clarity you have about your future vision, the easier it is for you to make the necessary decisions to move from where you are to where you want to be.

Idealize and *Imagine* Your Perfect Future

When we do strategic planning with an organization, we spend several hours encouraging the executives around the table to describe their perfect business sometime in the future. They imagine that they have all the time and money they need, and that they could create or shape the business in any way that they desire. What would it look like?

The answers that come back are almost always the same. The perfect business of the future would have excellent products and services, and an excellent reputation in the marketplace. They would have an excellent marketing system in place that generated a continuous stream of qualified customers for their products and services. They would have excellent sales systems, excellent customer service systems, excellent internal information systems, and high, consistent levels of profitability. They would have the best people at all levels, and be one of the most attractive places to work in their industry. They would be known far and wide as the quality leader in their business.

You then ask, "What will we have to do, starting today, to create the perfect business of the future?" This becomes your vision.

Then, continually ask, "What would have to happen for me to start moving from where I am today to create my ideal future vision of tomorrow?"

The *Ideal* Leader

If you were the perfect leader in your company sometime in the future, how would you be different from today? What is the first step you could take, right now, to begin becoming the person of your vision? What could you do to begin achieving personal excellence as a leader?

Each business and personal goal must be clear, written down, scheduled and measurable. Your goals must be so clear that a six-year-old could understand them clearly and tell you how close you were to achieving them. Your goals must be so clear that everyone in the company who is responsible for achieving any part of the goals is completely clear about what they are and how they will be measured.

Select One Key *Goal*

Here is a great question: *"What one business goal, if you were to achieve it, would have the greatest positive impact on your business?"*

Almost invariably, there is one goal, which if you achieved it, would have the greatest effect on your business. Every other goal is a sub-set of this major goal, and contributes to its achievement. What would the most important goal be for your business?

How will you measure success? What number would you use? In every business or career, there is invariably one number that is more predictive of success or failure than any other number. What is it for you, or for your business?

What is your deadline for achieving your most important goal? What are your sub-deadlines? How will you measure success at each step along the way?

Create a *Checklist*

To achieve any goal, small or large, you should create a checklist; *a series of steps organized by sequence to get from where you are today to where you want to be in the future.* This checklist becomes your blueprint, which you work on each day, and which everyone else works on as well.

A leader with a goal and a plan, and a team of people committed to achieving that goal, will accomplish five or ten times as much as another person or company that is not clear about where it wants to be sometime in the future.

Your ability as a leader to set clear goals, and create written plans of action to achieve them, in both your personal and business life, will determine how high you rise in leadership and responsibility. Your ability to set and achieve goals will determine your effectiveness and your success as a leader and as an individual for the rest of your career.

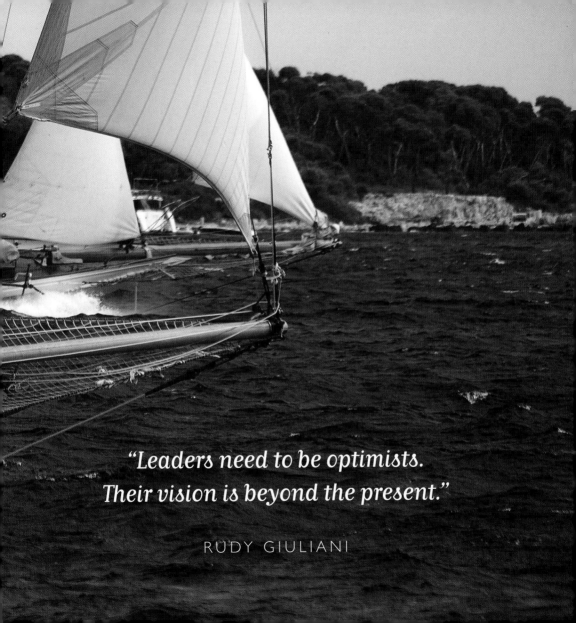

"Leaders need to be optimists.
Their vision is beyond the present."

RUDY GIULIANI

Leaders
Are Committed to Winning

The legendary football coach Vince Lombardi once said,
*"Winning is not the only thing; but **wanting** to win is."*

*Leaders are **ambitious**—perhaps the most important single quality in determining how far you go, and how fast you get there.* Leaders want to win. They want to be the best at what they do. They want to achieve victory. It is not possible to imagine a true leader in any area who is not committed to success in that area.

Leaders are highly competitive. They have a deep-down desire to succeed greatly at whatever they undertake. Leaders are committed to excellence, to personal excellence as individuals, and to business excellence in a competitive marketplace. They continually compare their performance with that of others, and continually raise the bar on themselves, striving to achieve at higher and higher levels.

"The quality of a person's life is in direct proportion to their commitment to excellence, regardless of their chosen field of endeavor."

VINCE LOMBARDI

Join The *Top 20* Percent

The top 20 percent of individuals in any industry earn 80 percent of the income and rewards in that industry. The top 20 percent of companies earn 80 percent of the profits in every industry, as well. As a leader, you should resolve today to join the top 20 percent in your field, no matter how hard you must work, or how long it takes.

Even better, commit to joining the top ten percent. Set this goal as a vision for yourself, of what is truly possible for you.

The good news is that everyone in the top ten percent or twenty percent today *started* in the bottom ten or twenty percent.

Everyone at the top started at the bottom. Everyone at the front of the line of life started at the back of the line.

And whatever hundreds or thousands, or even millions of others have done, you can do as well, if you are ambitious enough.

The bad news is that anything less than a life-long commitment to excellence becomes an unconscious acceptance of mediocrity, of poor performance. No company or individual ever started off with the goal of mediocre performance. But in the absence of a deep-down commitment to excellence, mediocre performance happens naturally and automatically.

Pay the Price

It takes a long time to become the best in your field, or in any field, but it is worth it. Most companies, and their first products and services, start off as average or poor quality. But because of the founder's commitment to excellence, they continually improve their product until it gets better and better, moving up in the customer satisfaction rankings. Eventually, they improve their quality so much that they become world leaders in their industries.

The satisfaction you enjoy by knowing that you are good at what you do, and that others recognize and respect you for it, is worth any price you pay in terms of time and discipline to achieve excellence.

Fortunately, there are only about five to seven key skills in any field that you must master personally to get into the top ten percent. And like a ladder, you climb these skill levels one step at a time.

Identify the Key Skill

Here is the great question in your attainment of personal excellence: *"What one skill, if you were excellent at it, consistently, would help you the most to advance in your career?"*

There is always one answer to this question, and you almost always know the answer, or you can find out by asking someone else. You may not be comfortable with the answer, with the skill that you need to develop to move ahead, but this discomfort is only because you have not yet mastered this particular skill.

The good news is that all business skills are learnable. Anyone who is excellent at any particular skill today, at one time could not do it at all. But they set it as a goal, they made a plan, and they worked on themselves and their business until they eventually became excellent in that area. And so can you.

Whatever the skill that you need to learn to move to the top in your business, write down the development of this skill as a goal, make a list of everything you will have to do to master this skill, set a deadline for achieving this skill, and then go to work to develop the skill.

Most importantly, take the first step. Buy a book, listen to an audio program, enroll in a seminar or workshop, and then practice, practice, practice.

The first step in anything new is the hardest step of all. Henry Ford once said that, *"The most difficult job is the one that you never get started on."*

Your willingness and ability, your discipline in taking the first step toward any goal, **especially a learning goal, is the starting point of all great success.**

"A journey of a thousand leagues begins with a single step."

CONFUCIUS

TAKE THE FIRST STEP.

Commit to Business *Excellence*

In business, fully 90 percent of your success will come from offering a *great* product or service in the first place. Whatever you sell, commit to becoming excellent in that product or service area. This means that you continually strive to get into the top ten percent in your field, based on customer opinions and satisfaction.

Most products and services start off at average quality or even below. But then, the leader makes a complete commitment to excellence, no matter how much it costs or how long it takes. The strategy for quality leadership is called,

"**CANEI**," which stands for "**C**ontinuous **A**nd **N**ever **E**nding **I**mprovement."

The Japanese call this system "Kaizen," which means *continuous betterment.* They attribute this commitment to never-ending quality improvement to the growth and success of modern Japan, and Japanese products.

To succeed in business, or in personal life, you must be *superior* to your competitors in at least one way, or in several ways. What is your area of competitive advantage in your products, services or overall business today? What should it be? What could it be?

In what important areas are your products or services superior to those of your competition? What could they be? What should they be?

What does your company do better for its customers than any other company in your industry?

In what areas could you be excellent? What will you have to do or offer to lead your field in the years ahead against determined competition?

The job of the leader in business is to choose the area of excellence, and then to get everyone in the business to strive for excellence in that area every day.

Customer *Satisfaction* is the Key

Tony Hsieh, president of Zappos.com, built a billion dollar business around the concept of offering superb customer service to people who bought shoes online. He said, "We are a customer service company that just happens to sell shoes." With that clear vision of customer service excellence, he built Zappos.com into the most successful company of its kind in the world, and sold it to Amazon.com for $1.2 billion dollars. His personal share was $400 million dollars.

The top ten percent of companies in every industry earn most of the profits in that industry. The reason for this is always because they are recognized as the quality leaders. And quality is always defined by the customer.

According to *Fortune* Magazine, the top leaders in business and industry today, the presidents of the Fortune 500 corporations, earn an average of 271 times that of the average employee in their companies. Why is this? It is mostly because they are recognized as the quality leaders in their fields as well. If one company did not hire and pay them that amount, because of their reputations as business leaders, they could walk across the street and get paid the same or more by another company.

Set a goal to be the best *personally* in your industry, and never stop working until you achieve it, no matter how many years it takes. In your position as a business leader, set a goal to make your company the best in its industry, as well. Commit to excellence in every area. Nothing can help you more to succeed in business than for you and your company to earn a reputation for excellence at everything you do.

"Excellence is to do a common thing in an uncommon way."

BOOKER T. WASHINGTON

*"Strive for excellence,
not perfection."*

H. JACKSON BROWN, JR.

Leaders Are Courageous

Winston Churchill wrote,

"Courage is rightly considered the foremost of the virtues, for upon it, all other virtues depend."

*The most common single quality of leaders is **vision**, a clear exciting picture of a desirable future.* The second most common quality of great leaders is *courage*, the courage to bring the vision into reality, to take action in the direction of their goals.

There are two parts of courage. The first is the courage to *begin*; to launch, to step out in faith toward your goal with no guarantee of success, and with a high probability of loss and temporary failure.

The second part of courage is the willingness to *endure*; to persist, to press on in the face of obstacles, setbacks and temporary failure. In both cases, the greatest obstacles are fears, of all kinds.

What holds people back from launching, from taking action to achieve their goals?

Overcome Your *Fears*

The greatest fears that most people have are the fear of failure, the fear of loss, poverty or embarrassment. These fears are the greatest blocks to success. Fear of *failure* paralyses action, distorts emotions, and causes people to hold back, or to make excuses for not going ahead.

But there are never any guarantees of success at anything. Failure, especially at the beginning of any new venture, is always possible, if not inevitable.

Leaders do not like to fail, but they realize that temporary failure is an essential part of the learning process. Business leaders repeat the mantras, "Fail fast, learn quickly, try again." And, "Do it, fix it, try it."

Successful people fail far more often than failures do. Failures are so terrified of loss that they try very little, or not at all, and achieve nothing as well. They seldom fail because they never take risks. They never try something new where failure is possible.

As it happens, top leaders are not impetuous, or risk-takers. They are instead "risk-avoiders" in the pursuit of profits and business success. The best leaders reduce the likelihood of failure by carefully evaluating every detail before they commit money and resources. They learn every detail of the situation or opportunity. They ask, "What could possibly go wrong?" They then make sure that those things that could go wrong, do not go wrong.

Confront Your Fears

The fact is that everyone is afraid. The courageous person is simply the person who acts in spite of his fear.

Mark Twain said, "Courage is not absence of fear; it is control of fear, mastery of fear."

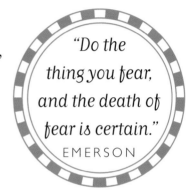

"Do the thing you fear, and the death of fear is certain."
EMERSON

The way to eliminate fear, and replace it with confidence, is to confront the fear, "face the fear and do it anyway."

Glenn Ford, the actor, once said, "If you do not do the thing you fear, the fear controls your life."

You develop the quality of courage by deciding exactly what you want, investigating the situation carefully, and then by taking definite, continuous, action in the direction of your goals.

The Iron *Quality* of Success

"Persistence is to the character of man as carbon is to steel."

NAPOLEON HILL

The second part of courage, the flip side of the willingness to launch, is *persistence*, the willingness to endure.

Once you have launched, and taken decisive action toward your goal, you will immediately experience setbacks, difficulties and potential failure.

This is the "testing time." This is the "persistence test" that nature sends you to see how badly you really want to achieve that goal.

Remember, difficulties come not to *obstruct*, but to *instruct*. Tony Robbins says that, "There is no such thing as failure; only results."

The key to developing persistence is simple but powerful. It is for you to make a decision, in advance, that no matter what happens, you will never give up.

Your ability to "preprogram" yourself is really quite extraordinary. By telling yourself that, "No matter what happens, I will never give up until I succeed," you plant the seeds of persistence that begin to grow deep inside your personality until you need them.

Then, when you face the inevitable setback or difficulty, your pre-programming will kick in, and you will bounce back. As my friend Charlie Jones used to say, "It is not how far you fall, but how high you bounce, that counts."

Leaders *Never Give Up*

Most successful people attribute their success to the fact that they would never give up in the face of temporary failure, no matter what the temptation. Eventually, through repetition and practice, they developed the habit of unshakable persistence that became a normal and natural part of their character and personality. They simply never gave up.

The keys to leadership success have always been two things. First, get started. Take the first step.

Second, keep going. Resolve in advance that you will never give up.

Orison Swett Marden, the founder of *Success* Magazine, and one of the most influential thinkers on success in American history, once wrote that, "The keys to success are simple: first, 'get-to-it-iveness,' and second, 'stick-to-it-ivness'." Aristotle said, "Both courage and persistence are habits learned by practice and repetition, over and over, until they become automatic ways of thinking and feeling."

When you practice acting courageously whenever courage is required from you, you will eventually reach the point where you become unstoppable, and your success will be guaranteed.

"We gain strength, and courage, and confidence by each
experience in which we really stop to look fear in the face...

we must do that which we think we cannot."

ELEANOR ROOSEVELT

*L*eaders
Get Results

Results are everything—in life, in business and in leadership. Leaders are those who have developed the ability to achieve the most important results expected of them in their positions. The first question of the leader is always, "What results are expected of me?"

The second question leaders ask is, "Of all the results that I can achieve, what are the most important results for my business?"

There will always be too much to do and too little time, especially for leaders in their positions of responsibility. All of life, therefore, consists of making choices and decisions between what is more important and what is less important, between what you care about the most and what you care about less.

The quality of your life today is a measure of the quality of your choices and decisions up to this point. To improve the quality of your life in the future, you must make better choices and different decisions in the present.

Use Your Time *Well*

Perhaps the most important decisions you make revolve around how you are going to allocate your time each day. Time management is really life management, management of yourself.

Time cannot be saved. It can only be spent differently. It can only be allocated away from activities of low value toward activities of higher value.

Ask yourself, "In what areas and activities can I achieve the highest return on my investment of time and energy?"

One of the key considerations for leaders has to do with the potential consequences of doing or not doing something. Something that is important is an activity that has serious potential *consequences* for doing it or not doing it. Something that is unimportant is something that has few or no consequences at all.

Top leaders focus and concentrate on activities that can have serious potential consequences for completion or non-completion.

Average people, those in the bottom 80 percent, may be as intelligent and as well educated, but they spend most of their time doing things that are fun and easy rather than things that are hard and necessary, and which can make a real difference in achieving key results.

Time Allocation for *Results*

There are two ways to think about how you spend your time as a leader. The first has to do with your *hourly rate.*

Leaders allocate their time in short amounts—hours, even the number of minutes they will spend on a task. The way you allocate your time in this sense is determined by the value of every minute and every hour that you invest. Your goal is to get the highest possible return on this investment.

> *"I recommend you take care of the minutes for the hours will take care of themselves."*
>
> LORD CHESTERFIELD

You determine your hourly rate by dividing your annual income—either your current income or your desired income—by 2,000—the number of working hours for people in the top ten or twenty percent of income each year.

If you earn $100,000 per year, divided by 2,000, this means that you earn $50 per hour.

The next step is for you to resolve not to do anything that does not pay you your desired hourly rate. Before you start a task, ask, "Would I pay someone else my hourly rate to do this task?"

If the answer is "No," refuse to do it. Delegate it, outsource it, delay or defer it, or eliminate it altogether.

Your time is your life, and it is too precious to waste on low-value, no-value activities.

The most important word in time management and leadership is **"CONTRIBUTION."** What contributions are required from you? Of all the contributions you can make, which is the most valuable?

The *Law* of Three

The second way to think about your time and your contribution is contained in the *"Law of Three."*

If you make a list of everything you do in a week or a month, you will probably come up with 20 to 30 different tasks and activities.

However, the Law of Three states that there are only three activities that represent 90 percent of the value of your contribution, and your income.

Use the three magic questions to determine your "Big three" activities:

1. "What one activity, if I did it all day long, would make the greatest contribution to my company and myself?"

Put a circle around this answer. **It will usually jump out at you from your list.** *Then, you ask:*

2. "What would be the second activity, if I did it all day long that would make the greatest contribution to my company?"

Put a circle around this task or activity as well. Then ask once more:

3. "If I could only do three things on this list, all day long, which would be number three?"

This answer may take a bit more time to find, but it will be clear.

What are the three most important and valuable tasks or activities you do in the course of your work in terms of the contribution you make and the value of the results you accomplish?

Once you have determined your three most important tasks, your goal must be to spend more time on each of them.

Here is the rule for leadership and personal success: *"Do fewer things, but do more important things, and do them more of the time, and get better at each one."*

Getting better at your key tasks is one of the best time management principles of all. By excelling at your most important tasks, you get more done, faster, and of a higher quality.

Keep asking yourself, *"Why am I on the payroll?"*

One of the most important questions in leadership is, *"What is the one thing that only I can do, that if done well, will make a real difference in my work?"*

Every day, every hour, there is one answer to that question, and by doing that before anything else, you will achieve more and better results, and make a greater contribution than in any other area of activity.

Your job as a leader is to focus *single-mindedly* on getting the most important and valued results expected of you in your position.

Your reputation for getting important results, consistently, is your key to getting paid more, promoted faster, and to realizing your full potential.

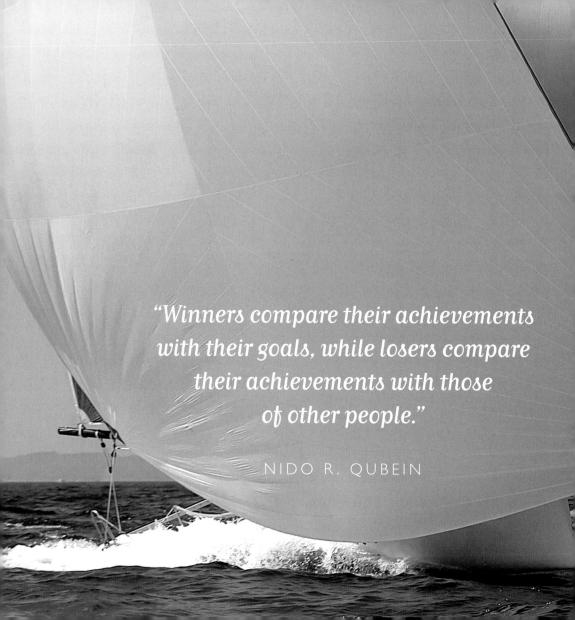

"Winners compare their achievements with their goals, while losers compare their achievements with those of other people."

NIDO R. QUBEIN

Leaders
Inspire Others

Peter Drucker wrote,

"The job of a leader is to get extraordinary results out of ordinary people."

Your most valuable assets are the people who report to you; the people who you depend upon to do the job and to get the results for which you are responsible.

According to studies, the average person works at about 50 percent of their true potential. Fully half of working time is spent in idle socializing, e-mailing back and forth, taking extended coffee and lunch breaks, reading the paper or on personal business.

A primary reason this time wastage occurs is because of poor management and "mal-organization."

This means that people are not deployed and directed to contribute their very best work to the company. And this is largely a leadership responsibility.

To inspire others, you must first be inspired and excited about the work yourself. You cannot give away what you do not have.

You must then transfer this emotion and excitement to others so that they feel committed and dedicated as well.

The Peak *Performance* Team

There are five keys to building a peak performance team of highly competent, motivated and inspired individuals. Here they are.

First, select your team members carefully. Fully 95 percent of your success as a manager or a leader will be determined by who you choose for your team in the first place.

Jim Collins, in his book, *Good to Great,* says that top leaders,

> "Get the right people on the bus,
> get the wrong people off the bus, and
> then get the **right people** into the *right seats* on the bus."

You can't build a peak performance team unless you have peak performance people. The existence of one negative or incompetent person on your team can undermine the morale and the spirit of the entire group.

Clarity Is *Essential*

"Good leaders must become what they want their followers to become."

LORD CHESTERFIELD

The second key to building a peak performance team is clear job descriptions. Each person must know exactly what he or she is expected to do, when it is expected to be done, to what level of quality, and how it will be measured.

In addition, each person must know what each other person does, and how each person's work affects each other person.

Get *Together* Regularly

The third key to inspiring people is for you to have regular meetings and discussions with your people, both one-on-one, and in groups, to review the work and talk about how to do it better. Top leaders are continually meeting with their people to share ideas and to learn about what is going on.

Top leaders and managers spend 75 percent of their time interacting with their team members; always looking for ways to help them do their jobs better. Poor leaders spend most of their time in their offices, busy with paperwork and phone calls.

Teach the Law of Three

The fourth key to building a peak performance team is to help each person identify the three things they do that represent 90 percent of the contribution that they make to your team or to the business.

Help them to focus and concentrate on those three tasks—and get them additional training to be even better in those areas.

There is nothing more motivating and inspiring than to be fully engaged in challenging, interesting work that makes a difference. A sense of accomplishment is the greatest single source of self-confidence and self-esteem.

Make People Feel *Important*

The fifth key to inspiring others is to build self-esteem in them continually. Make them feel important both as individuals and as employees.

There are six keys in the formula for making people feel important, motivating and inspiring them to give their very best to the company. The first five keys all start with the letter **"A."**

The first "A" stands for **acceptance.** Each person has a deep-down need to be accepted unconditionally by other people, especially the most important people in his or her life. When you unconditionally accept another person, without criticism, complaint or judgment, you make that person feel valuable and important, and inspire them to do their best work.

And how do you express unconditional acceptance toward another person? Simple. Just smile. When you smile at others, you raise their self-image, increase their self-esteem, and make them feel more valuable and important inside. This is why the very best and most productive bosses are also pleasant and positive people, smiling happily at their employees on a regular basis.

 The second "A" in making people feel important is **appreciation.** And how do you express appreciation? Simple: you say *"thank you"* on every occasion.

Whenever you thank others and express appreciation for anything that they have done, they feel more valuable and important. They feel more motivated and inspired to repeat the behavior. The words *thank you* are so powerful that you can use them continually, all day long, and no one will ever ask you to stop.

The third "A" in making people feel important is **admiration.** As Abraham Lincoln said, *"Everybody likes a compliment."*

> Whenever you admire the clothes or possessions of others, their home or office, or anything that they have achieved or accomplished, their self-image improves and their self-esteem goes up. They like themselves more. They feel more valuable and important. And because it is you who are making them feel so good about themselves, they like you as well and want to reciprocate by doing an excellent job for you.

The fourth "A" in the formula is **approval.** It is said that, "Children cry for it, and grown men die for it." Praise and approval are perhaps the two most powerful ways of building self-esteem and self-confidence in other people. In fact, another definition of the words self-esteem is the word "praiseworthy." Whenever people feel themselves to be worthy of praise by the important people in their worlds, they feel more valuable and important, and much more likely to repeat the behavior that was praised in the first place.

Be generous with your praise and approval. Praise people for their accomplishments, and for their attempts at various accomplishments. Praise people when they complete a task, and praise people when they complete part of a task.

To make your praise more powerful, make it both specific and immediate. Praise a person for a specific action, rather than generally. Praise them immediately after they perform the action, rather than later.

Because you are the leader, any praise coming from you has a *multiplier* effect on the person receiving the praise. Because you are a leader, your ability to give praise is a wonderful power that you have at your disposal to motivate and inspire others.

The fifth "A" in the self-esteem building formula is attention. Attention means that you listen carefully to people when they want to talk. Whenever people are listened to by their boss, or by someone who is above them on the ladder of life, they feel more valuable and important.

In fact, when you pay attention to another person, you are paying *value* to that person. This is why leaders have a high question to comment ratio. They ask twice as many questions as they make statements. They dominate the questioning and let the other person dominate the speaking.

Sometimes, the most powerful influence you can have in motivating and inspiring others is just to take time with them, ask them questions, listen intently to their answers, and praise their intelligence and their contribution.

The final key to inspiring others, number six, is for you to **build** *and* **maintain trust.** In annual surveys on what constitutes "a great place to work," trust is the most important ingredient mentioned.

Trust is defined by employees in terms of feeling safe and secure at work. They say, *"I feel that I can speak up, or make a mistake, and I will not be criticized or lose my job."*

As Steven Covey said, *"To be trusted, you must first be trustworthy." To truly inspire your people, you, too, must create a high-trust environment, a "great place to work."*

You will notice that none of the actions that you can take to motivate, inspire and make people feel valuable and important cost any money. What they do require is an awareness on your part of how your slightest word or gesture can raise or lower the level of performance and contribution of the people who look up to you for leadership.

The more you can build high-performing teams of peak performing people, the more results you will achieve and the more people will be entrusted to you to achieve even greater results in the future.

What actions could you take immediately to build greater self-esteem and self-confidence in your people?

"In the end, all business operations
can be reduced to three words:
people, product and profits.
Unless you've got a good team,
you can't do much with the other two."

LEE IACOCCA

Leaders Are Role Models

There are two main requirements for great success as a leader: competence and character.

Competence means that you are excellent at what you do, that you get consistent, predictable results, over and over again in your position.

Character is equally important, and perhaps even more so. Character means that you are known and respected for your *integrity*, that people can trust you, and believe in you, and feel confident that you will keep your word.

The most respected and honored men and women throughout history have been known for their characters, in addition to their achievements.

To inspire people, they must be inspired by your character and personality. They must see you as a role model. They must look up to you and want to emulate your best qualities.

Set *High* Standards

Perhaps the best question you can ask in becoming a role model is, *"What kind of a company would this company be if everyone in it was just like me?"*

At home, you can ask, *"What kind of a family would my family be if everyone in it was just like me?"*

As a member of your community, you can ask, *"What kind of a country would my country be if everyone in it was just like me?"*

If you are honest when you ask these questions, you will see that there are always a lot of areas where improvement is possible. Leaders are always open to the possibility that they could be better in one or more areas, and they are always striving to be better than they were before.

Set a *Good* Example

People will forget what you say, but they will remember what you do, the example you set with your behavior. Your example is more important in building your reputation than anything else.

Maya Angelou, the poet, once said, *"People will soon forget what you said but they will always remember how you made them feel."*

To lead by example, to be a role model of competence and character, is a never-ending job.

When you become a leader, everyone is watching you, judging you, and making decisions about you.

The "loneliness of command" refers to the fact that, when you become a leader, you no longer have the luxury of "letting it all hang out."

As a leader, you have a special responsibility to set and maintain high standards for yourself, and for others. This means that, if you want others to treat each other with respect and courtesy, you must treat everyone with respect and courtesy yourself.

Lead By Example

If you want people to focus and concentrate on their most valuable tasks, you must always work on your most important task yourself.

If you want others to be punctual, you must be punctual. Whatever you want others to do or be, you must lead the way. You must demonstrate the qualities that you want others to have.

"We must be the change that we want to see in the world."
GANDHI

The example you set as a leader has perhaps the greatest impact of all in the influence you have on others, and the eventual results of your team. Resolve today to be a man or woman of character and honor, one that others can confidently look up to and imitate, becoming better people in the process.

Your Leadership Potential Is *Unlimited*

When I was 24 and struggling, I made a profound discovery that changed my life forever. It dawned on me, like a revelation, that I could *learn* anything I needed to learn to achieve any goal I could set for myself. Wow!

This insight turned me into a "learning machine." I have read and studied an average of three hours every day since then, and sometimes six, eight or ten hours in a single day on a long airplane trip.

As a result, I went from a struggling salesman to a top salesman, and then to a sales manager and then to a sales executive, responsible for six countries. I went from the bottom to the top in less than two years, and became a leader in my industry.

Because I wanted to make the greatest contribution possible, I have read hundreds of books and thousands of articles on leadership over the years. And what I learned when I was 24 turned out to be true about leadership, as well.

You can learn anything you need to learn to become an excellent leader in your field. You can become one of the most important and significant people in your industry by learning and practicing key leadership principles, similar to what we have talked about in this book.

The wonderful thing about leadership is that your ability to grow as a leader never ends. You can continue to improve for your entire life. And as you get better on the inside in knowledge and understanding, your opportunities to be a more significant and important leader on the outside will continue to grow and increase.

By committing yourself to the seven secrets of exceptional leadership, you can become a better and better person, and eventually achieve all your goals as a leader in every area of your life.

Good Luck!

About the *Author*

Brian Tracy is one of the top leadership experts in the world today. His recent book, *How The Best Leaders Lead*, was singled out as "the best business book of the year" in 2011. He has spoken to more than 1,000 large corporations in 62 countries and 10,000 small and medium-sized companies in more than 5,000 talks and seminars on Leadership, Management, Personal Success and Business Development over the last 30 years. Brian has written more than 60 books that have been translated into 42 languages and sold in 65 countries. He has produced more than 500 audio and video learning programs which have been translated and distributed worldwide. This book, *The Seven Secrets of Exceptional Leadership*, describes the most important leadership qualities practiced by top leaders worldwide.

For more information on Brian Tracy, you can visit

www.briantracy.com

or call phone: 1-858-436-7300.

Or, write Brian Tracy International,

462 Stevens Ave., Suite 305, Solana Beach, CA 92075

What OTHERS are saying...

We purchased a Simple Truths' gift book for our conference in Lisbon, Spain. We also personalized it with a note on the first page about valuing innovation. I've never had such positive feedback on any gift we've given. People just keep talking about how much they valued the book and how perfectly it tied back to our conference message.

— **Michael R. Marcey,** Efficient Capital Management, LLC.

The small inspirational books by Simple Truths are amazing magic! They spark my spirit and energize my soul.

— **Jeff Hughes,** United Airlines

Mr. Anderson, ever since a friend of mine sent me the 212° movie online, I have become a raving fan of Simple Truths. I love and appreciate the positive messages your products convey and I have found many ways to use them. Thank you for your vision.

— **Patrick Shaughnessy,** AVI Communications, Inc.